The American Traveling Carnival

By

Kenneth L. Miller

millerbooks, llc
Chicago

Forward

The American traveling carnival arose from a frontier need for entertainment, a depression inspired need for gambling and a Victorian era desire to let off steam. Economic and social repression gave way to traveling safety zones where almost anything went. The story of the carnival reflects the story of America from the late 1800's to where we are now.

In this essay, and in my book *Steele's Amusements, Carnival Life on the Midway*, (now available on Amazon.com) I describe the social and structural framework for the modern carnival and a specific case in *Steele's Amusements*.

In researching the historical foundation of this very American institution, I relied heavily on resources available at the Chicago History Museum, (chicagohistory.org) and the Newberry Library also in Chicago. (newberry.org) These research facilities are available to the public for free or for a nominal charge; thus the library and museum deserve your support. Consider a donation to each of them.

This topic encompasses a wide swath of American social history, and I recommend each of the sources cited in the *Notes*.

For your consideration, I give you a sample of a most fascinating subject. I hope you enjoy it. I also encourage your feedback via email: kmiller@triton.net

Kenneth Miller

1893

"The World's Fair, like all exhibitions, is a striking example of imprudence and hypocrisy: Everything is done for profit and amusement...from boredom...but noble aims of the people are ascribed to it. Orgies are better." -Leo Tolstoy, 1893

The World's Columbian Exposition of 1893 was Chicago's great coming out party. A mere twenty-two years after a fire that wiped its geography clean, Chicago was back in a very big way. The population was expanding at a break-neck pace and the economy of corruption was doing a good job of keeping up. Money was pouring into Chicago, and the con artists, gamblers, and thugs followed along. During the six months of the fair, 27,529,400 people found their way to the 'Windy City.'[1] They heard the call of hyperbole, and succumbed to the promise of an American

4

utopia. What the attendees found was a land of great contradiction and greater illusion.

The fair was split into two distinct areas: From the lakefront arose a Daniel Burnham inspired dream of massive white buildings, lagoons with electric boats, and technological wonders too new to have recognizable names. This was the 'White City.' The buildings were covered in a white plaster material called 'staff' and glistened in the sunlight along the western shore of Lake Michigan. Some were the largest structures ever built by man, but only gave the illusion of permanence. The thin white coating applied over a framework was never meant to last past October 30, 1893. The buildings didn't last, but we live with the legacy of the fair over a century later.

The White City had ascribed to it noble aims, as Tolstoy said, but the other fair, the separate show along the Midway Plaisance, stretching from the lakefront westward into the city of Chicago was indeed an orgy. From 1893 onward, the word 'midway' would mean one thing to most people. It refers to that most American invention, the traveling carnival.

1893 was a year of contrasts. Like 1929, the economy had formed a bubble. Business was running white-hot and it looked like there would be no end to the opportunities available. The World's Columbian Exposition formed the country's largest public works project. Chicago had rebuilt all the buildings lost in the great fire of 1871 and built more and built them bigger and better. People flowed into Chicago to work in the building trades and the population exploded. In 1893, the census reached over one million for the first time. Chicago became the second largest city to New York in population, surpassing Philadelphia. It was a pivotal year and a year of endings and beginnings. Peter Tchaikovsky died in 1893, but artist Joan Miro and actors Mary Pickford, Leslie Howard (Gone with the Wind) and Andy, of Amos and Andy were born in that same year. Bad guy Nazi, Hermann Goering was born in 1893, but good guy Jimmy ("the Schnoz") Durante was also born that year and lived to the ripe old age of eighty-six. 1893 was a good year for the Ford family. Edsel Ford was born and his father, Henry built his first gas-powered automobile in 1893. It was a good year for automotive competition as well, since Rudolf Diesel published plans of his revolutionary invention, the Diesel engine in 1893. The first open-heart surgery was performed by an African-American doctor, Daniel Hale Williams in 1893, which should have been a great feather in Chicago's cap, but the operation was to remove a knife from the heart of a street brawler in the most corrupt and dangerous city in America. Some had dampened enthusiasm for the surgical achievement, wondering why it should have been needed or done anyway. Rutherford B. Hayes, the nineteenth president of the United States died in 1893, but Mao Tse Tung and Huey Long were both born that year, making for some interesting politics to come. Pope Leo XIII was in the Vatican in 1893 to write encyclicals and Lizzie Borden was in jail for whacking her parents. Remember the rhyme? "Lizzie Borden took an axe and gave her mother forty whacks. And when she saw what she had done, gave her father forty-one." Lizzie Borden was acquitted in 1893 and Mae West was born in Brooklyn that year. Jack the Ripper was fairly quiet in 1893, but Chicago's H.H. Holmes was just getting started as America's most famous serial killer. Abner Doubleday, the 'father of baseball' died in 1893, the same year that Japan adopted the Gregorian calendar, on which they placed baseball as their favorite sporting event.

Most importantly for the purposes of this work, the American traveling carnival was born in Chicago on May 1, 1893 with the opening of the World's Columbian Exposition, and a mere twenty three days earlier, from a dirt floored house in Indiana, L. E. Steele was brought into the world. L. E. Steele would form the quintessential traveling carnival, Steele's Amusements.

The traveling carnival grew from a unique set of conditions and social components present in Chicago in 1893. Chicago was the epicenter of a perfect cultural storm: The World's Fair was a magnetic force drawing a rapid influx of cheap labor to work in the building and service trades. Tens of thousands of people were lured into the city hoping for jobs, and seeking a glimpse of the future. As the fair building came to a close, the rise of unemployed workers and the influx of independent showmen formed an atmosphere of desperate need. The unemployed needed to fill their stomachs and the showmen needed customers also known as marks. Couple this atmosphere with a degree of political instability and corruption. Chicago became a volatile city: A cultural powder keg. The economic crisis known as the Panic of 1893 further added to the incentive workers needed to find new work, new industry and a way out. The ubiquitous presence of vice, gambling, con men, thugs, murderers, and thieves formed a complex and dangerous system for newcomers to navigate. Frequent warnings appeared in the Chicago Daily Tribune of the perils of crowds thronging the elevated platforms. On July 1, 1893 the Tribune described a typical day of World's Fair robberies: "Thieves worked the crowd at the Elevated Station...as a result, Dr. J.H. Albright of Denver lost $200 in bills and diamonds worth $800. Another man said that he had been robbed of his pocketbook containing $500, and a woman lost a valuable gold watch."[2] Something had to give and Chicago was bursting with an unholy energy from which revolution might evolve. In fact, the instability and political unrest was of great concern to the newly elected (for the fifth time) mayor, Carter H. Harrison, Sr. His inaugural address on April 17 let all present know just how hairy things had become:

"It has been spread broadcast over this land, and has even crossed the briny deep, that the electorate that has chosen your Chief Magistrate was an electorate of thieves , thugs, gamblers, and disreputables. We stand before the world with a black mark upon our character. Let it be your and my endeavor to wipe this slander out and prove to the world that Chicago is a city governed by its best people, and that its Mayor and its Common Council govern it on principles of business and respectability."[3]

--Carter H. Harrison, Mayor of Chicago, 1893

* * *

Harrison knew only too well the corruption that had brought him to office...again. His reputation for being soft on and, in fact, nurturing of vice in Chicago was the stuff of legend. As much as he decried the reputation of Chicago as being a stewpot of gambling, prostitution and accompanying political corruption, he was it's longstanding cultural architect. Like mayors before him, he soft-pedaled enforcement of the vice laws. As an example, the Chicago Daily Tribune in August of 1893 reported a "Raid on Gamblers". As the result of a special grand jury, eighty-seven indictments were handed down for various gambling house keepers, dealers, and associated criminals. No one was particularly worried about the consequences of these legal actions. This was Chicago, and the indictments were window dressing. All the gambling establishments continued in operation, unabated and many of the indictments were considered flawed and unlikely to be successfully prosecuted. Mayor Harrison predicted a failure (of the crackdown) and stated that "(He) does not think these low dives can be stamped out."[4] The mayor had made his prophecy self-fulfilling by not having the police aid State's Attorney Kern in the bust. The ready supply of gamblers and gaming structure was an important part of the World's Columbian Exposition and of carnivals thereafter. Though not an official part of the fair, the gambling and vice just outside the gate on Cottage Grove had made its mark. Carnivals carried with them games of chance and developed an ongoing reputation for being "Cheap, tawdry and not quite honest."[5]

This influx of people from the countryside, looking for work and adventure came to Chicago to build the fair, but when the job was done, so was the steady pay. The next component of future traveling carnivals fell into place: A relatively unskilled, unemployed workforce with few alternatives was on the loose. They could become prey to the corrupt and violent society of late 19th century Chicago, or find a niche in that society and move on.

The unrest that developed from masses of unsettled workers allowed anarchists, labor organizers, and agent provocateurs to advance their causes. Chicago was and is a political city and the politicians in place in 1893 didn't want to lose control. On August 8, 1893 Mayor Harrison was quoted, "There are 200,000 people in Chicago today unemployed and almost destitute of money. If Congress does not give us money, we will have riots that will shake this country."[6] It's not uncommon for a Chicago mayor to rattle Washington for more money, but Harrison was seriously worried about stability in wake of the World's Fair. The unemployed were not necessarily voters and the next mayoral election was two years off. But still, civil unrest was at an all time high. The danger was not to the ballot box, but rather of angry mobs torching the fair, the city, or both.

The sources of the unemployed were varied. Many had come to Chicago to work in the building trades, lost their work and remained in the city. During the height of unemployment in 1893, the bars were feeding

60,000 people per day for free.[7] This was Chicago's version of the social safety net. By the end of July 1893 the Chicago Daily Tribune had reported, "Idle men Pouring In."[8] Men by the thousands were arriving daily by train boxcar from the closed mines of Colorado. They sought work harvesting crops and some still thought the fair would be hiring workers. They were wrong. The men had to eke out a living on the streets of Chicago however they could. 1893 had hosted the second economic depression of the century and like depressions before and after, served as inspiration for survival and ingenuity. Joining a carnival meant survival.

Before 1893, the disparate elements of the traveling carnival had not yet been fused into a single operating unit. There had been many sideshows; most notably those promoted by P.T. Barnum that moved across the country displaying a combination of human, animal and archeological oddities, but not integrated outdoor amusements like that of the World's Fair. Americans had become enamored with the unusual and foreign, and P.T. Barnum traveled far and wide to find the objects of their fascination. The allure of "Otherness" became the reason for throngs to surge into Chicago. Under the guise of Ethnology, the study of people through their divisions of race and geographic distribution, the World's Fair was to bring in whole villages of people from Africa, Asia, the Pacific and the Americas. At this point in post-civil war history, the separation of colored people's exhibits on the Midway Plaisance from the European and Anglo-Saxon exhibits of the 'White City' was considered a sign that

America had remained a racist country. Frederick Douglas and Ida B. Wells gave speeches and wrote of this division in a pamphlet, "*The Reason Why the Colored American Is Not in The World's Columbian Exposition.*" The issue was somewhat diffused by critics who pointed out that the division of cultures between the White City and the Midway Plaisance was not that of race, because on the midway, the Austrian village was next to the Dahomey village and the Japanese bazaar was next to the Dutch settlement and German village. The Midway Plaisance and therefore the genesis of carnivals in general started as a cultural amalgam. Douglass and Wells spent a little too much time stewing over the discrimination of the White City and missed the cultural progress brewing along and just outside of the midway. From 1893 it became a carnival axiom that diversity was a carnival's most marketable commodity. Paying customers wanted to see something different; as radically different as possible and they wanted to be entertained. A carnival manager would never exclude an act based on race, but only on the basis of interest, uniqueness or marketability. After all, this was now the entertainment business. Fast forward to the twentieth century, Steele's Amusements, from the strikingly white environment of Valparaiso, Indiana included a black sideshow act billed as "Baby Flo Johnson". "We've got Baby Flo Johnson! Alive! Alive! Alive! She's so big, she's so round it takes ten men to hug 'er and a boxcar to lug 'er! She's 816 pounds of screamin' big fat Detroit Soul Mama! Come in and see her ALIVE!" Her color was not relevant in the context of what she brought to the show, other than it provided yet another valuable facet of 'Otherness'. In a sense, the carnival sideshow was the perfect example of color-blind merit employment. From the standpoint of the carnival business, personal views of race were set aside in favor of promoting marketable product.

Traveling minstrel shows had toured Europe for centuries combining musical entertainment with freak shows and oddities. The minstrels were the predecessors to the carnival sideshow and the carnival sideshow became an essential cog in the carnival wheel. All traveling carnivals must have three essential elements: Riding devices, shows or exhibits and concessions and gaming. From 1893 onward, the three traveled together as a unit named after the Midway Plaisance in Chicago: The Carnival Midway.

"Midways became an essential part of all subsequent fairs in America and of smaller versions of Americas carnivals and sideshows; No fairground, however insignificant was complete without one."[9]

After the World's Fair, carnivals became "bound together by a degree of overlapping membership for some of its practitioners and common news coverage in and communication through common specialized periodicals..."[10] The carnival magazine, *Billboard* appeared and served as a central organizational tool for carnies to use. Traveling carnivals would find employees, techniques, equipment and solace in the pages of their journal. Eventually, *Billboard* became *Amusement Business* but folded in 2006 after 111 years of publication.

Two of the carnival elements were brought to Chicago as part of Burnham's grand design: rides and exhibitions. The third, gaming component was something that just showed up along with the incoming showmen.

When the financing fell through for the Easton Tower and Restaurant, a 560-ft. tall tower, the Exposition lost its most spectacular piece. In order for the fair to compete with the memory of the 1889 Paris show and Eiffel Tower, Burnham would have to come up with something else quickly.

Enter Carnival element: The Ferris Wheel. George Washington Ferris was a young engineer and bridge builder from Pittsburgh, Pennsylvania. He had heard Burnham's challenge to come up *not* with something of "mere bigness" but a truly original and distinctive engineering fete. The reputation and prestige of American civil engineers was at stake and more importantly, the French had to be bested after their 1889 Eiffel Tower stunt. The Eiffel was after all a magnificent piece of engineering, but it was static: perfectly designed to be emulated in souvenir paperweights for centuries to come. Ferris's mind tended to the kinetic. His creation would at once be a magnificent technological achievement and a moving one, rendering the Eiffel Tower yesterday's news. The Paris fair had introduced the Eiffel Tower to 28 million visitors. With Ferris's help, Chicago's fair would surpass Paris in all metrics including size, grandeur, complexity and most importantly, commercial success. The Paris "Exposition Universelle" of 1889 covered 95 hectares or 235 acres. The Chicago Fair would dwarf Paris's in area by covering 1037 acres. The entire World's

Columbian Exposition would be lit by electric lights and powered by steam. And, although the Chicago Fair's technological fete, the Ferris Wheel would be 'less tall' than the Eiffel Tower, it would heist 1368 passengers aloft three times per hour, bringing in revenue to exceed $726,000.[11] Fairs then, and carnivals to come had become all about the money and all about surpassing any previous success. Indisputably, the Chicago fair had done that.

The Ferris Wheel was without question the first substantial and universally recognizable carnival ride. But another attraction of the World's Columbian Exposition held an important position in carnival history. Nestled between the American Indian Village and the Chinese Village and Theatre on the Midway Plaisance, the Captive Balloon Ride rose 1500 feet above the crowds to view the White City and the less clean-looking City of Chicago. For two dollars, a ticket holder could ride higher than even the Eiffel Tower and see Michigan, Indiana, Wisconsin and a little more of Illinois. The French-made balloon contained 100,000 cubic feet of hydrogen gas that was manufactured right in the park. The Captive Balloon ride was an important reminder of the carnival's most underrated attraction: risk of death. On July 10, 1893 a powerful windstorm raked over the World's Fair, striking the Captive Balloon. The giant "gas bag" was shredded and dropped pieces of silk one-half mile in all directions. Luckily, the quick thinking ride manager (as opposed to the "aeronaut" that rode the thing up) ordered the balloon securely tethered and emptied of passengers before the worst wind hit. No injuries were attributed to the balloon ride save for a woman that fainted when the wind at 1000 feet picked up during her ride. Wind and lightening are two dangers that carnival operators live with or die by. In 1893 the wind didn't affect the Ferris Wheel, but blew right through it. Future carny ride operators would always have to weigh the risk of a lightning strike on a tall metal ride versus the benefit of a full load of paying customers. Usually, the customers won out.

Concurrently with the World's Fair, Chicago's economic boom was teetering on the brink of catastrophe. The gold reserves that backed the U.S. dollar had fallen below the $100 M benchmark and by spring of 1893, several key banks had to close their doors. Bank customers, fearing that their paper money was no longer redeemable for gold began to panic and made runs on the banks that remained open. The Chemical National Bank of Chicago locked out depositors in May and by the end of the crisis, 575 banks had halted operations. The economic ripple effects were felt across the nation. The railroads started to go under in February with the closure of the Philadelphia and Reading Railroad. The country's most actively traded stock; the National Cordage Company went into receivership. The stock market tanked in March and April and eventually 15,000 businesses failed. The Northern Pacific Railway, the Union Pacific Railroad and the Atchison, Topeka and Santa Fe Railroads all failed.

By July, amid news that the crisis was abating, the Erie Railroad failed. Renewed panic followed until September when the banks started to allow full withdrawals of cash by depositors. The great Panic of 1893 played out almost entirely within the time frame of the World's Columbian Exposition. The glee and pride that America felt in the run-up to the Chicago fair had the gut wrenching side affect of economic fear. The throngs of country folk that came to Chicago to seek a better life found themselves trapped in a dangerous city in the midst of economic collapse. And the band played on.

The carnival continues to survive through the worst of times as diversion from reality and the success of the World's Columbian Exposition of 1893 was a prime example of a depression proof business. This example was not lost on the crowds of unemployed workers huddled in vacant lots near the World's fair. "In 1892, independent showmen by the scores came into Chicago. The streets were jammed with thousands of construction workers employed on the exhibition grounds. Ideal customers for showmen sat upon vacant lots around the downtown area."[12] The great unwashed and undereducated began to set up adjunct businesses outside the gates of the Exposition on 63rd Street. On Cottage Grove Avenue and outside of the Buffalo Bill's Wild West Show, vendors provided services and amusements not found inside the White City or anywhere else decent people gathered.

"A little Ferris Wheel, and still a littler one, work their unlovely motions in that vast and unlovely region that has fastened to the Fair on Cottage Grove Avenue--a huge barnacle of entertainment, avarice and sin..."[13] -John McGovern, editor of *Illustrated World's Fair*

The Chicago Tribune ran front-page articles complaining about the robbery and vice outside the gates of the Exposition. Complain as they would, it was inevitable that these vices would become an integral part of the carnival experience.

Those that moved on into the carnival life had to take what was offered, subsistence, but it also offered something else of great value: "The carnival was a non-judgmental environment where the deformed, the drifter, the loser, could find a place that would accept him unconditionally; it was a metaphor for freedom from troubles, from the mundane, and into a magical world where the rule is that things aren't always what they seem. The carnival was the poor man's entertainment."[14] For the carny, the carnival was a supportive family. By the end of May, 1893 the first-ever national meeting of carnival showmen had taken place in Chicago. The carnies ascertained that the midway needed more sex appeal and decided to push the belly dancing or "danse du ventre"[15] What a crowd-pleaser that turned out to be. It turned the 'Streets of Cairo' section of the midway into an international sensation. Songs were written, including the "Cairo Street Waltz" dedicated to the exhibit's managers.[16] The famous midway promoter, Sol Bloom felt that the most popular attractions would be Oriental dancers in burlesque shows, while admitting that most of the girls were from Iowa and corn-fed.[17] The midway showmen, it was reported, put up a preacher to condemn the publicly indecent dancing. The crowds swelled for the forbidden. Continuing the illusion, the showmen introduced Fatima the exotic Middle Eastern dancer. The crowd was thrilled with the (unknown to them) female impersonator. By 1933 Fatima was a father of five and a grandfather of seven.[18]

The showmen's relentless promotion of attractions along the midway via the "ballyhoo" or carnival talk caused the fair management some consternation. Fearing that the constant hawking would scare off some of the wholesome crowd, ballyhooing was for a time prohibited.

"Here's your goody Bum-Bum Candy...Nice Bum-Bum Candy"[19]

--A simple ballyhoo from a candy vendor along Cairo Street in 1893

The showmen, being an inventive lot developed a system of mute hand gestures to pull in the crowds and the midway continued to do business until the ballyhoo ban was deemed unenforceable. Carnivals have honed the ballyhoo talking skill since its inception at the World's Fair. The carnival "talk" has been handed down through oral tradition and now been translated, taped, digitized, and commoditized yet remains a carnival's most important point-of-sale marketing. Not only did carnivals develop a rich linguistic addition to the English language, but a secret, simple code to communicate on the commercial battlefield. Sometime in the early twentieth century, carnival folk invented "czarny", a pigeon English slang that served as code when communication needed to be disguised. Czarny is another piece of the carnival oral tradition that has survived through generations of showmen.

Along with a ready workforce, the carnival adopted the gambling component or more aptly, the gamblers latched on to the carnival and wouldn't let go. Asbury in his classic, *Gem of the Prairie* described the scene..."Chicago was the most wide open town that America had ever seen or probably ever will see. And it was, also, with the exception of New York in the days of Boss Tweed, the most corrupt and, for that matter had been for a decade."[20] The World's Fair provided a ready supply of victims for the Windy City to grind up and was " ...a boon to sneak thieves and pick-pockets."[21] So at the time of the fair, in this environment, shakedown artists like Mickey Finn operated with impunity. Finn was a 'lush worker' that would rob drunken men along the rough area of south Clark Street. With a sign posted inviting newcomers to, "Try a Mickey Finn Special" the unsuspecting fair goer would get more than he bargained for. The famous Mickey Finn consisted of raw alcohol, water from soaked snuff and a dash of chloral hydrate. The victim would take a slug, fall into a stupor and maybe revive in eight hours if Mickey had gotten the dose right. If not, and frequently he did not, the fleeced and stripped victim never awoke and was found in a back alley, dead. For the beer drinkers, Mickey had devised the 'Number Two', which contained beer instead of the pure grain alcohol, but had largely the same effect.[22]

Also at the time of the fair, vice, always a staple of Chicago life kicked into high gear. "At Carrie Watson's brothel, "...the girls, 20-30 ordinarily, but twice that many during the World's Fair, received company in diaphanous silk, and performed their ancient rites upon sheets of finest linen."[23] Gambling and prostitution had risen to such a degree that international attention was drawn to it. From this attention, men of the cloth traveled from afar to minister to the modern day Gomorrah. One minister, William Stead made quite a name for himself by writing a 1894 book called, "If Christ Came to Chicago." He based his analysis of Chicago and his plea for temperance on a one-month visit to the World's Fair near its end. In this volume, Stead set out to expose the entire sordid sinful story of Chicago. The book included a detailed map of the red light districts, saloons, brothels, and gambling houses. Following the law of unintended consequences, Stead's book became somewhat of a travel guidebook for the adventuresome, showing exactly where vice could be found and patronized.

The fair created another American hero and grist for dime novels and pulp, the super-cop. Not the Wyatt Earp of Western fame, but an urban sleuth and crime fighter, Detective Clifton Wooldridge found his calling at the World's Fair. His morality was clear from the statement: "In these houses could be found every low and demoralizing phase of life that a human mind could think of." Detective Wooldridge set out to corral the criminal element and racked up an impressive record of 19,500 arrests.[24] This achievement was set down in his 1901 memoir, *Hands Up!* The fair and Wooldridge's exploits spawned a genre of popular detective fiction: *Against Odds: A Detective Story* by Emma Murdoch Van DeVenter,

Chicago Charlie, the Columbian Detective by John Harvey Whitson and *Joe Phoenix in Chicago* by Albert Aiken were examples of the dime novel pulp that the fair launched.[25]

When P.T. Barnum was consulted in the planning stages of the World's Columbian Exposition, the goal was to form a wider demographic appeal for the fair, an appeal to the lower classes.[26] Barnum contributed ideas for structure and layout of the midway, but his biggest contribution was that of expectation and promotion. P.T. Barnum was the promoter of the Greatest Show on Earth and to that end his recommendation published in an essay was that the fair organizers should, "Make it (The World's Columbian Exposition) the Greatest Show on Earth, -- greater than my own Great Moral Show -- if you can."[27] On Barnum's advice, promotional packets were sent worldwide. "Among the activities promoted to the school officials (all across America) was the suggestion that the school day begin with a "pledge of allegiance to the flag", the text specially written as part of the Fair's promotional materials."[28]

The suggested layout of the Midway Plaisance was a plan that would last for over one hundred years. The first carnival midway in 1893 right on through to the midway of Steele's Amusements in 1976 had a similar, logical, P.T. Barnum scheme: A long boulevard lined on each side by attractions. Entrances at one or both ends of the midway lead ticket holders to attractions in the center or opposite end. At the World's

Columbian Exposition, the center attraction or "draw" was the Ferris Wheel. The entire Midway Plaisance was arranged around an a-la-carte menu of concessions, rides, and amusements. This pay as you go system did not set well with the high minded of 1893, however. "Unlike the White City, the Midway bustled with commerce and consumption."[29] The thought of accepting *filthy lucre* in exchange for amusement was distasteful and served as a discordant counterpoint to the classy displays of the White City. Again the precedent was set for carnivals to come: By taking money at individual games, concessions and exhibits on the midway, carnival organizers could bring in independent showmen and concessionaires. These independents acted as separate businesses, paying "privilege" or rent to the manager. A century later, most carnivals are still organized this way.

At the World's Columbian Exposition, 370 concession permits were sold.[30] Individual companies were formed to handle many of the complicated and expensive rides and exhibits. The Captive Balloon ride on the Midway Plaisance had a large number of shareholders and was incorporated as the World's Fair Captive Balloon Company. It operated as an independent business and suffered its losses independently as well. Fast forward to the twentieth century Steele's Amusements: Certain rides and exhibits were owned, co-owned, shared and set up as separate businesses. The carnival became a group of cooperating interests working within a business framework.

The appeal of survival through jobs, appeal of entertainment through amusements and games and the appeal of a promise for the future through exhibitions and architecture brought throngs of people to the city. America's first recorded economic depression in 1879 was still fresh in the planners' minds, and the memory of the Paris Exposition was that even with the Eiffel Tower, the fair was only marginally successful. Chicago's fair would have to do better than Paris. On Chicago Day, October 9, 1893 the fair brought in 716,881 attendees and proved that Chicago's success would eclipse Paris and guarantee a profit for the organizers. The final cost of the World's Columbian Exposition came in at $33,401,543 thus showing a profit, showing up Paris and showing the world that Chicago had come back, twenty-two years after the fire that was thought to level the city for its sins.

Notes to The American Traveling Carnival:

1)   Marion Shaw, <u>World's Fair Notes</u>, Pogo Press, 1992

2)   "Pick Pockets Rob Fair Visitors," Chicago Daily Tribune July 10, 1893 p.1

3)   Inaugural Addresses of the Mayors of Chicago: Mayor Carter H. Harrison, Sr. April 17, 1893, Journal of   Proceedings, Chicago City Council   p. 40-41

4)   "Raid on Gamblers," Chicago Daily Tribune, August 24, 1893, p. 1

5)   Truzzi, Marcello, and Easto, "Carnivals, Roadshows and Freaks," Society 1972 9(5): p.26-34

6)   "Mayor Harrison Expects Labor Riots," Chicago Daily Tribune, August 9, 1893, p.1

7)   Herbert Asbury, <u>Gem of the Prairie</u>, p.155

8)   "Idle Men Pouring In," Chicago Daily Tribune, July 31, 1893, p.1

9)   Philip McGowan, <u>American Carnival-Seeing and Reading American Culture</u>, Greenwood Press,   Westport, CT, 2001 p.24

10)   Truzzi, Marcello, and Easto, p.26-34

11)   Joe McKennon, <u>A Pictorial History of the American Carnival</u>, Popular Press, Bowling Green, OH 1972,   p.30

12)   Ibid., p.23

13)   Ibid., p.35

14)   Michael Baers, Traveling Carnivals, Gale Encyclopedia of Popular Culture, St. James

15)   Norman Bolotin, Christine Laing, The World's Columbian Exposition, Preservation Press, Washington   D.C. 1992 p.130

16)   Neil Harris, Grand Illusions, Chicago Historical Society, 1993

17)   Justus Doenecke, "Myths, Machines and Markets, : The Columbian Exposition of 1893" the Journal of   Popular Culture 1973 4(3) p.53

18)   Joe McKennon, p.34

19)   Chicago Times Portfolio of the Midway Types, American Eng. Co. Publishers, Chicago 1893

20)   Herbert Asbury, p.170

21)   Herbert Asbury, p.172

22)   Herbert Asbury, p.175

23)   Herbert Asbury, p.137

24)   Herbert Asbury, p.126

25)   Donald Hartman, Fairground Fiction, Detective Stories of the World's Columbian Exposition, Motif   Press, 1992

26)   Philip McGowan, p.24

27)   P.T. Barnum, "What the Fair Should Be," North American Review 150   (March, 1890)

28)   Aileen Forman, "Meet Me at the Fair! The World's Columbian Exposition Showed the Best of America   to the World," collectingchannel.com

29)   Neil Harris, p.123

30)   James Doolin, 1893 Columbian Exposition, Admission and Concession Tickets," Doolco, Inc., Dallas, TX   1981 p.1

For more information, visit:

steelesamusements.com

and

millerbooks.com

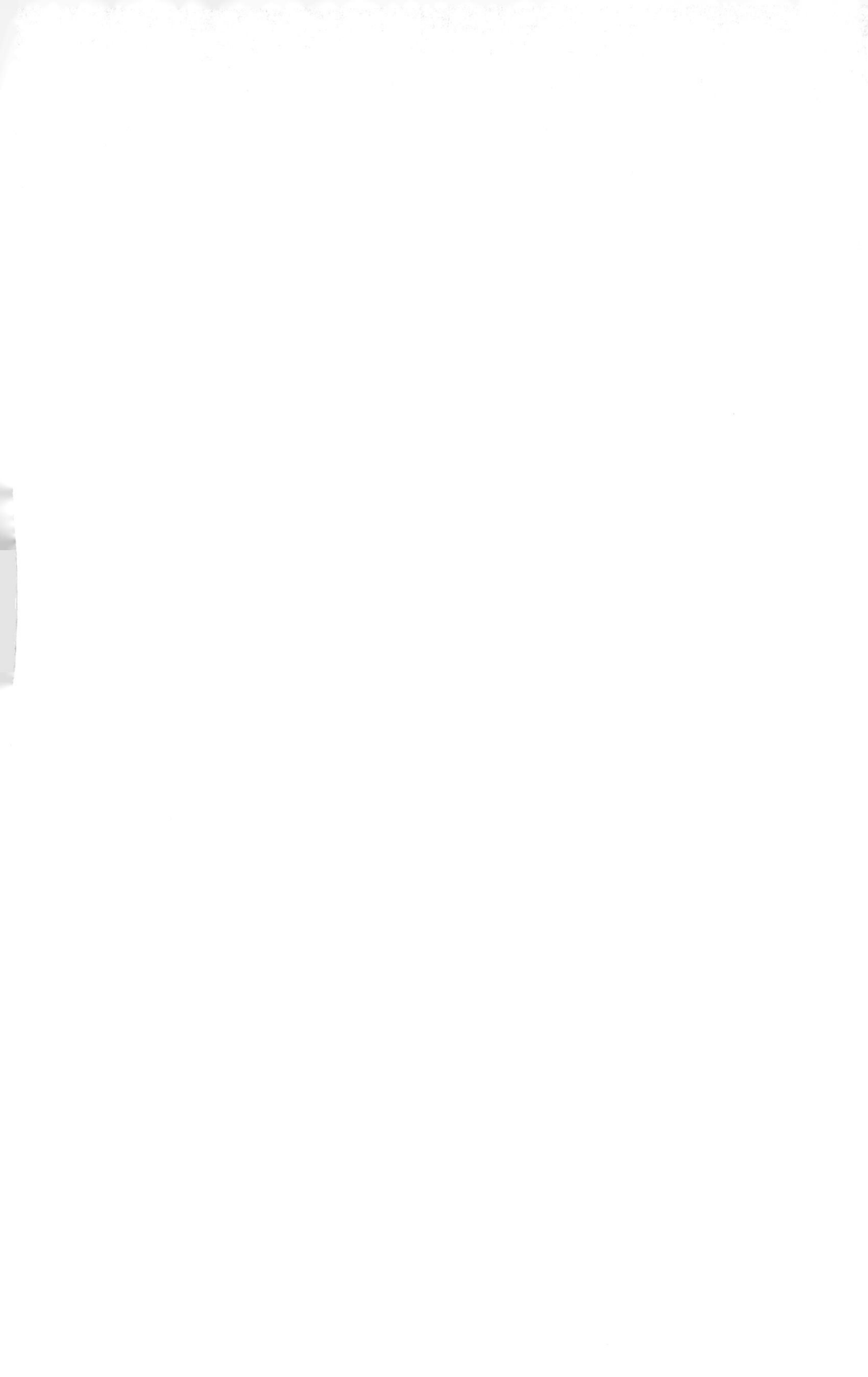

www.ingramcontent.com/pod-product-compliance
Lightning Source LLC
Chambersburg PA
CBHW021123020426
42331CB00004B/609